Cottage Garden

✺

A JOURNAL

by JACKIE BENNETT

Illustrated by ANNY EVASON

FRIEDMAN/FAIRFAX
PUBLISHERS

CONTENTS

❧❧

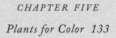

CHAPTER ONE

Cottage Gardens Past

*T*he cottage garden was not invented at any particular date; it developed naturally, out of a combination of necessity and desire—the necessity for small landholders to produce enough food and flowers for their own families and the desire to make their gardens the envy of their neighbors. Everyone has his or her own mental picture of what a cottage garden should be. For most, there should be a path winding to the front door through borders of sweet-smelling hollyhocks *(Alcea rosea)*, lavender *(Lavandula)*, and pinks *(Dianthus)*. The door should be framed by an old-fashioned rose, or a scrambling honeysuckle *(Lonicera)*, and every available space should be packed with plants that either look good, taste delicious, or smell heavenly.

❧❧

*T*he first cottage plots didn't always fulfil the romantic notion of later years. The medieval cottager was much more likely to have a pig, a few ducks, an apple tree, and a cabbage patch than a garden full of flowers, but it wasn't long before cottage gardeners were growing a much greater diversity of plants, such as herbs, flowers, and fruit. Thomas Tusser's *One Hundred Good Points of Husbandry*, written in 1557, recommended cornflowers *(Centaurea cyanus)*, love-in-a-mist *(Nigella damascena)*, marigolds *(Calendula officinalis)*, sweet Williams *(Dianthus barbatus)*, and violets *(Viola)*, as well as asparagus, red mint *(Mentha gentilis)*, sage *(Salvia officinalis)*, sorrel *(Rumex acetosa)*, and tarragon *(Artemesia dracunculus)* for the kitchen—quite a cosmopolitan selection even by today's standards.

From the 16th century onward, cottage gardening ceased to be confined to the garden, and plants were cultivated in pots on the cottage windowsill and grown for cut flowers for jugs and vases. The first windowsill flowers were lavender, lilies *(Lilium)*, marigolds, pinks, roses *(Rosa)*, stocks *(Matthiola)*, and violets, but by the 18th and 19th centuries, the range had extended to include fuchsias, scented geraniums *(Pelargonium)*, hydrangeas, mimulus, and saxifrages.

*M*any plants found their way into cottage gardens via farm hands who, after a day toiling in the fields, would return to their homes carrying cuttings, bulbs, and seeds of flowers they had seen growing in the countryside. Columbines *(Aquilegia)*, cornflowers *(Centaurea)*, cowslips *(Primula veris)*, daffodils *(Narcissus)*, foxgloves *(Digitalis)*, poppies *(Papaver)*, primroses *(Primula vulgaris)*, snowdrops *(Galanthus)*, and violets owe their garden origins to the curiosity of early cottagers. The 19th-century English farm laborer-turned-poet, John Clare, who roamed the villages and countryside around his Northamptonshire home, saw this happening in his own neighborhood, and wrote:

> *"The Cottager when coming home from plough*
> *Brings home a cowslip root in flower to set."*

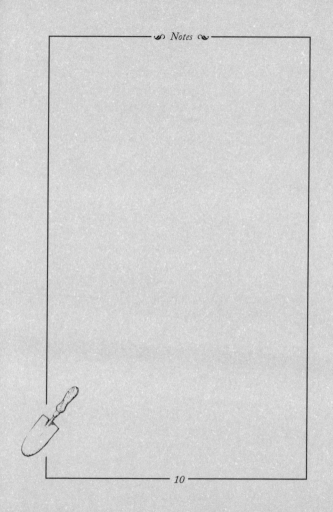

*C*ottage gardeners in the 19th century were the unwitting conservationists of their day. They had neither the money nor the opportunity to join the craze for plant hunting that was sweeping the Western world, so they carried on cultivating and nurturing the old-fashioned flowers that were rapidly losing popularity. Unlike well-to-do gardeners, cottagers could not afford to buy exotic shrubs and tender bedding plants, and as a result, cottage gardens preserved many hardy plants, such as faced pansies *(Viola)*, pinks, polyanthus, and the perennial climbing pea *(Lathyrus latifolius)*, which might otherwise have died out. Nursery catalogs of the 19th century listed hundreds of different varieties of these flowers, but by the beginning of the 20th century, the lists had shrunk to only a handful of names.

↪↩

*B*eekeeping and the production of honey were essential cottage-garden industries, providing the households with their only source of sweetening. There is nothing more satisfying than watching bees "'working" the plants, and cottage gardens were full of bee-friendly plants, such as borage *(Borago officinalis)*, lavender, mignonette *(Reseda odorata)*, red valerian *(Centranthus ruber)*, and wild thyme *(Thymus serpyllum)*. Bees will roam more than half a mile from their hives in search of nectar, so it is more than likely that cottagers were providing flower-filled gardens for their neighbors' bees, rather than their own. Planting for bees served a dual purpose, because in foraging for nectar, the bees also pollinated the flowers.

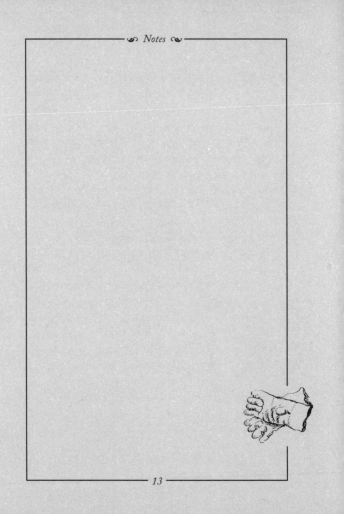

The Madonna lily *(L. candidum)* can possibly lay claim to being one of the oldest plants in existence. It appears on Cretan vases of the Minoan period (around 1700BC), and was well known to the Phoenicians, the Assyrians, and the Romans. To cottage gardeners Madonna lilies were so commonplace that they were grown in rows, rather like vegetables. Throughout the centuries, the bulbs have been used as fodder for cattle, to make poultices for cuts and scalds, and even as a cure for baldness, but the plant's greatest asset, and that which makes it one of the best-loved of all lilies, is its scent—a sweet, heady perfume that fills the evening air. Madonna lilies can be tricky to cultivate, and are best planted 1in (2.5cm) deep in late summer, rather than in fall (autumn), when other lilies are planted. They prefer a rich, moist soil in full sun.

*A*nother of the oldest bulbs to be found in gardens is the poet's narcissus *(N. poeticus)*. Its history stretches back to the times of the Ancient Greeks, who, being renowned for their learned poetry, were perhaps responsible for giving it its romantic name. The flower is very distinctive, with white petals and a central red "eye", and can still be found growing wild in Greece and Spain. In the garden, it likes a moist soil, and naturalizes well in grass. One variety, *(N. p.* var. *recurvus)* best known as old pheasant's eye, has become a cottage-garden favorite.

William Shakespeare loved all spring flowers, but his favorites were the daffodils, which he described so lyrically in *A Winter's Tale*:

> *"Daffodils*
> *That come before the swallow dares, and take*
> *The winds of March with beauty."*

The daffodils about which he wrote were most probably the dainty, deep-yellow, wild daffodils of England (*N. pseudonarcissus*), which were so prevalent in Elizabethan times. Today, they can still be found growing in a few locations, but have been superseded, to a great extent, by bigger and bolder garden hybrids.

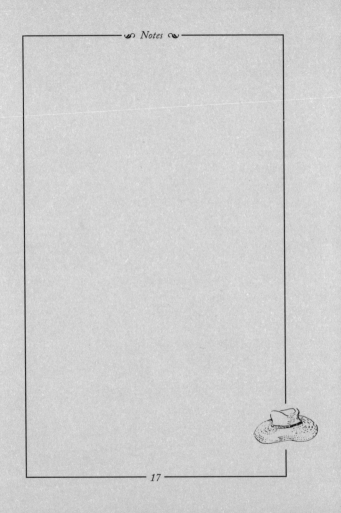

Primroses are not only pretty, they have a fascinating history too. Wild primroses do best in the dappled shade of a damp woodland or on the banks of a stream, but thanks to the old cottage gardeners who so loved them that they bred garden varieties, we now have primroses that can be grown in open borders. Double-flowered varieties were very popular in the 16th century, and gardeners believed that if single-flowered plants were dug up and transplanted regularly, they would produce double flowers. Eventually, however, cottagers tired of the plants' simple, cream and yellow colors, and were overjoyed when a pink form, the "Turkie purple," was introduced from Turkey. From here it was a short step to producing the polyanthus, a cross between a primrose and a cowslip, with a longer stalk, and multi-flowered head. Today, there are so many multi-colored forms, that it is hard to believe they all originated from the humble yellow primrose.

❧❧

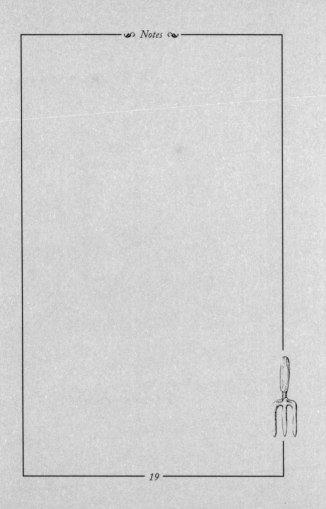

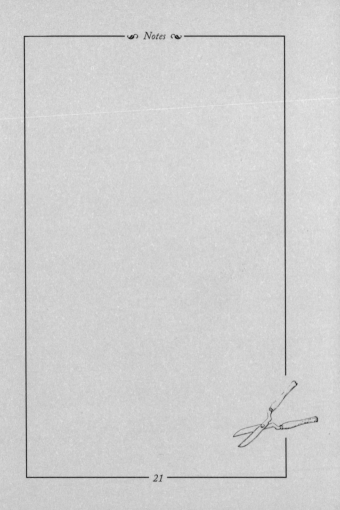

Aquilegia vulgaris

Aquilegia alpina

Aquilegia 'Nora Barlow'

Columbines are mentioned in most early books on cottage gardening. They are authentic cottage flowers, first gathered from the wild, then gradually introduced into the flower border. The wild columbine has violet-blue flowers, and, once established in the garden, will hybridize freely with other varieties. It self-seeds prolifically, and a few plants sown in the garden should be enough to produce an array of unexpected and interesting varieties each year. Some of the old varieties are still grown, particularly 'Nora Barlow', which was named after the granddaughter of Charles Darwin, and 'Munstead White', now called 'Nivea', which was a favorite of Gertrude Jekyll, the doyenne of cottage gardeners in Edwardian England. In the 19th century, varieties with long, swept-back "spurs" were developed from *A. caerulea*, the state flower of Colorado, and a native of the Rocky Mountains. These long-spurred hybrids are the most popular columbines grown in gardens today. The name columbine is derived from the Latin *columba*—a dove—and the swept-back petals are thought to resemble birds' wings. In some places, the plants are known as doves-at-the-fountain.

One of the oldest roses still in existence is the apothecary's rose (*R. gallica* var. *officinalis*), which was grown in the monasteries and physic gardens of medieval Europe. In the 13th century, it was known as the rose of Provins, because the monks of Provins, near Paris, made a famous conserve from the hips, and the scented petals were used in the perfume industry in the same area. The deep pink, semidouble flowers hold their fragrance longer than most other roses, and they became an essential ingredient of potpourri. Closely related to the apothecary's rose, 'Rosa Mundi' (*R. g.* var. *versicolor*), is the crimson-and-white striped rose that legend says was named after "fair Rosamund," the mistress of Henry II of England. Both these roses are ideal if you want a hardy, fragrant hedge.

∾∾

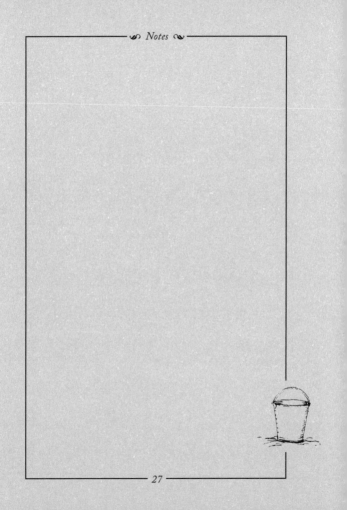

*F*or a vivid picture of the traditional cottage garden, look no further than the poet John Clare, who wrote without sentimentality or exaggeration. He describes perfectly the cottage and its garden, making readers dream of recreating the scene in their own gardens:

> *"Where rustic taste at leisure trimly weaves*
> *The rose and straggling woodbine to the eaves,*
> *And on the crowded spot that pales enclose*
> *The white and scarlet daisy rears in rows,*
> *Training the trailing peas in bunches neat,*
> *Perfuming evening with a luscious sweet,*
> *And sunflowers planted for their gilded show,*
> *That scale the window's lattice ere they blow."*

*I*n the early 20th century, the garden at Hidcote manor in Gloucestershire, England, was laid out by its owner, Lawrence Johnston, and it became the archetypal cottage garden on a grand scale. By using hedges to divide up the space and create a feeling of enclosure and protection, Johnston allowed scope for a more relaxed style of planting than had been seen for many years under the prim Victorians. Fuchsias, hydrangeas, peonies, and primulas were planted randomly instead of in formal swathes. Annual flowers were allowed to self-seed freely around the garden, and climbers, such as honeysuckles, clematis, and vines, were allowed to scramble over hedges and walls. For the first time, the gentry were becoming as relaxed about their gardens as the country people had always been.

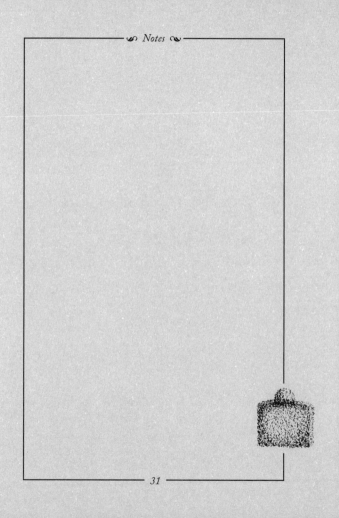

CHAPTER TWO

Planning a Cottage Garden

"What is the secret of the cottage garden's charm? Cottage gardeners are good to their plots, and in the course of years they make them fertile ... But there is something more and it is the absence of any pretentious 'plan', which lets the flowers tell their story to the heart."

William Robinson, 1883

𝒲illiam Robinson recognized that the essence of a cottage garden was its simplicity and its artlessness. The look to aim for is one where the garden appears to be unplanned but has, in reality, been thought out and planted quite carefully, and has the perfect combination of natural planting and subtle structure. A cottage garden is neither full of hard landscaping and high-tech gadgets, nor an untended plot of unruly plants. Achieving just the right balance is the art and the craft of cottage gardening.

Notes

Fences, Hedges, and Walls

*B*oundaries are one of the first considerations for any garden. Fences, hedges, and walls are all suitable, and a cottage garden will blossom within any of these confines. For most of us, the decision will have been made by some previous occupant of our home, but if you have a choice, it is best to try to fit in with your surroundings—look around your neighborhood, and go with the local consensus, whether it is for green hedges, painted picket fences, or stone walls.

*I*n a small garden, the boundary has to be functional as well as attractive, and that is why old cottage-garden hedges were often of fruit bushes or small, espalier apple trees. These "living hedges" served the dual purpose of providing shelter for the plants and fruit for the cottager. Rose bushes also make good, multipurpose hedging, providing scented flowers in summer, hips in fall, and a thorny barrier all year round. Eglanteria/ sweet briar *(R. eglanteria)* is the traditional cottage hedging rose, with single pink flowers followed by huge orange-red hips, but *R. rugosa rubra* or *R.* 'Roseraie de l'Hay' also make good hedges. For year-round coverage, golden privet (*Ligustrum ovalifolium* 'Aureum') is bright and cheerful even in the darkest winter.

∽∾

*T*raditional fencing, or "dead hedging," as cottagers used to call it, was often constructed from wooden pickets or pales, painted to match the color of the house or left natural, with a small gate at the bottom of a path opposite the front door. A picket fence will last for many years if you erect it carefully and secure it to stout upright posts. Alternatively, you could use wattle hurdles made from woven willow or hazel, which look natural. In country areas, you may find craftsmen who can make the hurdles for you, but if not, they are available in ready-made 6ft (2m) panels from garden centers. Wattle fencing is not intended to be very long lasting, but it makes an attractive and rustic boundary, nonetheless.

∾∾

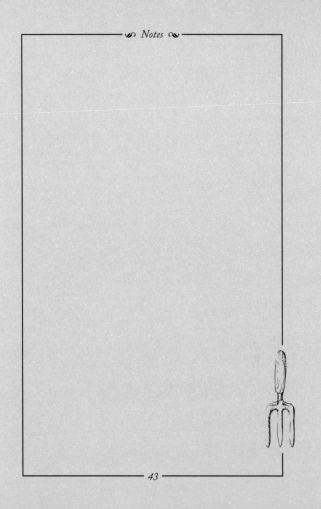

Arches and Pergolas

*I*n a small garden, climbing plants help to make use of all the available space. Many old cottages had rose-covered wooden porches or verandas where the family could relax at the end of the day, and the idea of roses growing around the door has become the epitome of cottage gardening.

In the garden itself, it is quite simple to erect a free-standing arch or pergola, either to mark the transition from one part of the garden to another—from flower garden to vegetable garden, for example—or simply as a way of growing your favorite climbing plants. There is no need for the structure to be ornate because it will be hidden by the plants. Choose a rustic material, such as rough-hewn timber, or wrought iron if you like, but a ready-made arch in light tubular steel is easy to erect, and will not look out of place when it is covered with plants. Whatever material you use, an arch or pergola must be strong enough to take the weight of the plants, and wide and high enough for people to pass through it without becoming entangled. A width of 4ft (1.2m) and a height of 7ft (2.15m) is about right.

*R*oses are the most popular choice of climbers for arches, and with a little care will give years of pleasure. The choice of roses is vast, but ramblers with flexible stems are best. *R.* 'Albertine' is a fragrant pink rambler that will eventually reach a height of about 15ft (5m), which is more than enough to clothe an arch. *R.* 'Seagull' is a small-flowered, white rose that will grow to 20ft (6m). When you have planted the rose, mulch the soil around it and twine the stems around the upright posts of the arch. In the first summer, pinch out the top shoots of the leading stem to encourage branching farther down. That way, the rose will completely cover the arch with foliage and flowers.

❧❧

Paths

*C*ottage-garden paths can be both functional and ornamental. You will need a path that leads from the front door to the gate, and another from the back porch to the tool shed or greenhouse, but you can also use paths for visual effect—one that winds gently through a narrow garden, for example, will help to create an illusion of width. Before you lay any paths, you will need to decide on the most suitable type for your garden, and for the purpose for which it will be used. Grass paths look very natural in a country garden, and can be a solution if the flower beds are to be dug out of an existing lawn. They will need regular mowing, of course, and can become muddy in winter, but they are inexpensive and attractive. Gravel is also inexpensive, and can look very attractive if you match the color of the stones to the surrounding buildings. Use stones that are at least ½ in (1.2cm) in diameter, as they are less likely to be kicked around the garden, or carried into the house on people's shoes. Old bricks make excellent paths, particularly if the house is also of brick. Lay them, set out in a decorative herringbone or basket-weave pattern, on a bed of hardcore and sand.

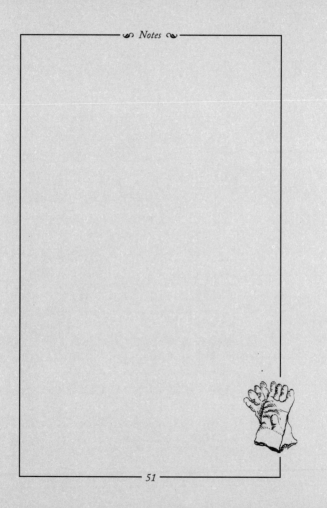

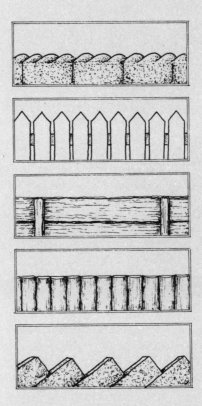

Edging

*Y*ou can choose from a variety of materials to edge the paths and borders in a cottage garden. It is important to use edging in a subtle way that won't spoil the informal look of the garden–old bricks, tiles, timber strips, and logs can create the right effect. Bricks can either be laid end-to-end or sunk into the ground at a 30° angle. Rope-top and other decorative edging tiles are very popular in town gardens. Sink them into the soil to two-thirds of their depth. Wooden edging should be treated with a preservative to prolong its life.

*A*s an alternative to hard edging, you can use plants to delineate paths and features. A single row of pinks or thrift *(Armeria maritima)* planted on each side of a path can look very attractive, as can an edging of dwarf lavender or silver-leaved lavender cotton *(Santolina chamaecyparissus)*. To borrow an idea often seen in more formal gardens, plant rows of boxwood *(Buxus sempervirens* 'Suffruticosa') at 9in (23cm) intervals to create a compact, dwarf, evergreen hedge. These neat edges make the perfect framework for an informal planting scheme and give the garden an air of maturity.

Containers

Cottage gardening in containers is the solution if you have only limited space—or no garden at all. Cottagers have always enjoyed growing plants in whatever containers were available. The type of container doesn't matter at all, what matters is that it is planted to overflow with flowers.

Let your imagination run riot and scour the house and garden for unusual items to use as containers. Old cooking pots, earthenware jars, enamelware, wicker baskets, chimney pots, tin pails, wooden barrels, old sinks and troughs, and metal or wooden wheelbarrows can all be given a new lease of life as interesting homes for plants. Give baskets a coat of waterproof varnish to prolong their lives before you plant them up.

*F*or a cottage windowsill, use a wooden box stained or painted to match the house or the window frames. Drill a few drainage holes in the base and cover these with broken crockery. Add a layer of gravel to improve drainage and half-fill the box with potting mix. Add trailing plants, such as dwarf nasturtiums *(Tropaoleum majus)* or ivy-leaved geraniums, to soften the edge of the box. At the back and center, plant dwarf tobacco plants *(Nicotiana)* and small wallflowers *(Cheiranthus)* for fragrance, and blue-flowered bellflowers *(Campanula carpatica)* for color and coverage. Surround the plants with more potting mix, firm it in well, and water thoroughly.

Plant up an old stone trough or sink to make a miniature cottage garden. Most of the old cottage favorites are available in dwarf varieties, which are ideal for growing in containers. Place the trough or sink in its permanent position before you plant it—it will be too heavy to move when it is filled with potting mix and plants—and choose a place where it will be in sunlight for most of the day. Add a layer of drainage material—gravel is best—then fill with potting mix. Plant an assortment of small cottage-garden plants, such as bellflowers, columbines, diascias, double daisies *(Bellis perennis)*, phlox *(P. subulata)*, pinks, and thrift. The foliage and flowers will soon spread out to make the sink garden look as if it has been there for many years.

❧❧

*T*opiary

*T*opiary—yew or boxwood hedges clipped into a variety of interesting shapes—is very attractive in the garden, but the trees can take years to grow and may need special clipping. A quicker, easier, and less expensive alternative is to train ivy to grow over hoops of wire. Plant two or three small trailing ivies in a large terra-cotta pot. Insert the wire framework

(diamonds, hoops, or globes are the simplest shapes to start with), making sure it is firmly anchored in the potting mix, then gently twist the stems of the ivies around the wires to produce instant topiary.

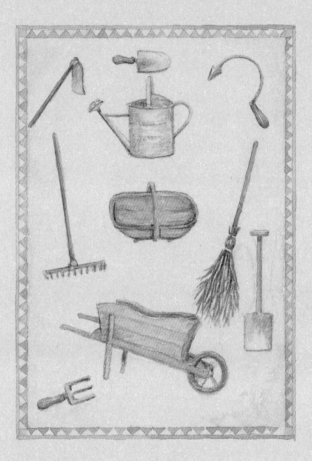

Making Virtues of Necessities

You will need a place to keep things such as tools and flowerpots, and space for at least one compost bin. If your garden is very small and you are reluctant to give up part of it to a utility area, the answer is not to hide the "business end" of the garden from sight, but to choose materials that will complement it rather than clash with it.

Frost-proof terra-cotta pots can be stacked outdoors to leave room in a shed for expensive tools. Traditional slatted-wood compost bins look attractive, are the best choice for recycling waste, and will help to keep the garden tidy by conveniently storing clippings, lawn mowings, and prunings. If you have the space, a double bin is ideal; it allows you to leave one heap of compost to mature while you are making the next.

Compost

By following a few basic principles, you can turn your garden and kitchen waste into sweet-smelling nutrients for your soil. Most garden waste can be composted, including dead flowers, old bedding plants, hedge clippings, fallen leaves, lawn mowings, and annual weeds. You can also add kitchen scraps, such as vegetable peelings and tea leaves. Don't put perennial weeds, such as ground elder, bindweed, couch grass, or dandelions on the heap, and avoid annual weeds that have set seed, unless you can be sure that the heat of the heap will be sufficient to kill them. Otherwise, they will germinate as soon as you spread the compost on the garden. Add the material to the heap in layers, and chop up woody stems or put them through a garden shredder to help them break down more quickly. Include a layer of farmyard manure, or sprinkle on some high-nitrogen activator, which you can buy from garden centers. If the heap is very dry, moisten it a little with water, then covered it with a lid, or a piece of old carpet to keep the rain out and the heat in. Turn the heap after 6-8 weeks, and the compost should be ready to use in 4-6 months.

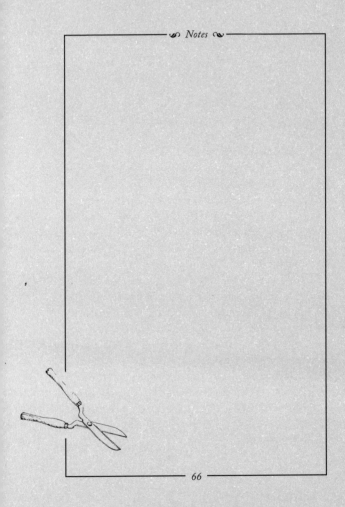

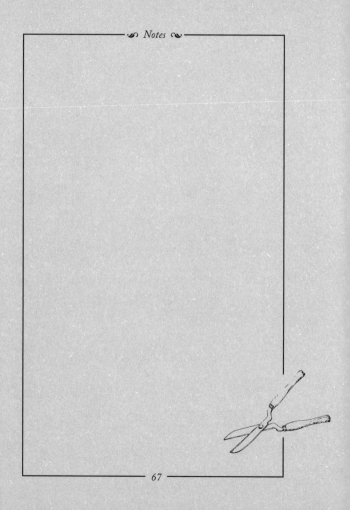

CHAPTER THREE

Plants for Scent

*W*hen we think of a cottage garden, we think of romantic summer days filled with the sounds of bees at work and the sweet scent of old-fashioned flowers. A cottage garden would simply not be a cottage garden without scented plants. During the day, lilies, pinks, roses, and stocks are rivals for the best perfume, while at dusk, evening primroses *(Oenothera biennis)*, night-scented stock, climbing honeysuckles, and summer jasmines have their hour of glory.

Pinks

Old-fashioned garden pinks were the cottagers' first choice for perfume. John Parkinson, 17th-century author of the first illustrated book on ornamental plants, could hardly find the words to express his admiration:

"What shall I say to the Queen of delight and of flowers, Carnations and Gillyflowers, whose bravery, variety and sweet smell, tyeth every one's affection?"

Gillyflower is the old name for members of the Dianthus family, derived from the French *giroflier*—a clove tree. Many of the old-fashioned pinks were clove-scented including the famous 'Sops-in-Wine' variety, which has single, maroon flowers with white markings, and was grown around taverns and alehouses so that the petals could be used to flavor the liquor.

*P*inks are still the favorites of most gardeners, and few plants have their qualities of "bravery" (hardiness), compactness, perfume, and show of pretty flowers from early to midsummer. Set out new plants in spring, 12in (30cm) apart, and water them well. Pinks like a sunny position in well-drained soil, and will benefit from a top dressing of gravel to prevent the bases of the plants from coming into contact with damp soil. You can take cuttings after the flowers have finished–choose strong shoots and cut them off close to the main stem. In late summer, remove the old flower stems and apply a high-potash fertilizer.

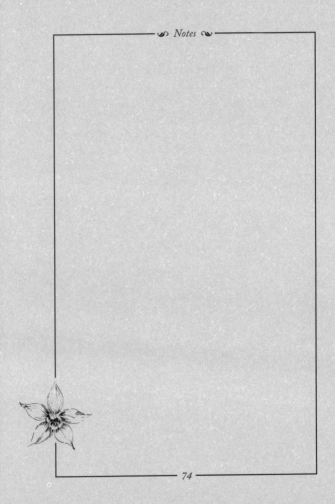

Scent in Small Spaces

Even the tiniest garden can be planted for perfume–all you need is a small border and space on the patio for a few containers. At the back of the border, put in one or two old Alfred de Dalinas garden roses, such as *R.* 'Mousseline' or 'Gloire de France', or plant a compact mock orange, such as *Philadelphus* 'Manteau d'Hermine'. At the front, plant lavender, lemon verbena *(Aloysia triphylla)*, pinks, and violets, and add pots of scented geraniums.

❧

Plants for Potpourri

A well-planned scented garden can provide lots of material for indoor flower arrangements and potpourri. The ingredients for potpourri are a matter of personal preference, but rose petals are usually the basic ingredient, to which herbs, pinks, and scented-leaved plants are added. The secret of making a successful potpourri is to pick the leaves and petals when they are in peak condition, on a dry day, and lay them out in a warm, dry, place, out of direct sunlight. You can dry small quantities in an old-fashioned flour sieve or a garden sieve. Turn the leaves and petals frequently to make sure they dry thoroughly, then store them in cardboard cartons or dark-colored glass jars until you have enough to make the potpourri.

❧❧

A traditional recipe for potpourri:
1 cup rose petals, ½ cup petals from clove-scented pinks, ¼ cup each of marjoram and rosemary leaves, 1 teaspoon ground cloves. Mix thoroughly and place in china bowls or specially made potpourri containers.

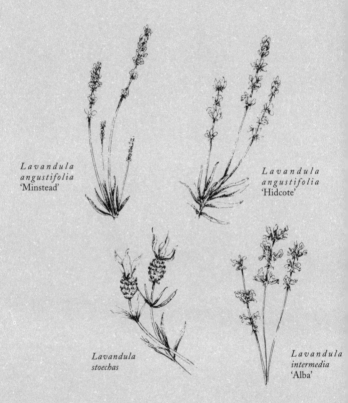

*Lavandula
angustifolia*
'Minstead'

*Lavandula
angustifolia*
'Hidcote'

*Lavandula
stoechas*

*Lavandula
intermedia*
'Alba'

Lavender

Lavender is a great delight wherever it is planted in the garden. It is easy to grow if it is given good drainage and an open, sunny position, and it makes a good companion for roses. It looks especially good grown as a low hedge or as a path edging, but it can also be included in a mixed border of shrubs and herbaceous perennials. If your soil is moisture-retentive or heavy, dig in plenty of grit or horticultural sand before planting. The best time to put out young plants is in early spring, by which time, hopefully, they will have missed the heaviest downpours of winter rain. The species or variety of lavender you choose will depend on where you intend to plant it. Tall bushes, up to 4ft (1.2m), are good for hedging or for growing toward the back of a border. The dwarf varieties are best for edging paths. For an unusual, two-tiered effect, plant a row of tall-growing bushes behind a row of dwarfs. One of the oldest varieties of lavender is *L.* x *intermedia* 'Grappenhall', which has been a cottage- garden favorite since the late 18th century. French lavender *(L. stoechas)* has unusual, tufted flower heads. Lightly clip over the lavender in fall to remove dead flower heads and to keep the bushes from becoming straggly.

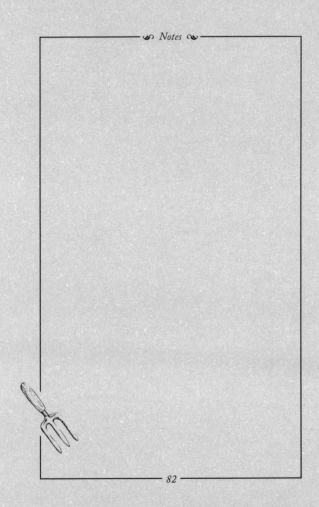

$\mathcal{M}$ignonette (*Reseda odorata*) is another essential in the cottage garden, but when you look at it, with its ordinary green leaves and beige flowers, it's hard to imagine why. The answer, of course, is the wonderful scent that drifts from the plant on warm summer evenings, particularly after a shower of rain. This delightfully fragrant plant is an annual, and was introduced to France from North Africa in the 18th century, where it caught the imagination of romantic gardeners, who gave it the name mignonette, meaning little darling. Traditionally, it was also grown as an indoor pot plant in winter. For winter flowers, sow the seeds in late summer in 6in, or 15cm pots of potting mix, and place them in a cold frame or greenhouse. Thin out the seedlings to leave three in each pot, and pinch out the growing tips to encourage bushy growth. In late fall, bring the pots indoors to a well-lit place where the flowers will fill the house with their wonderful aroma.

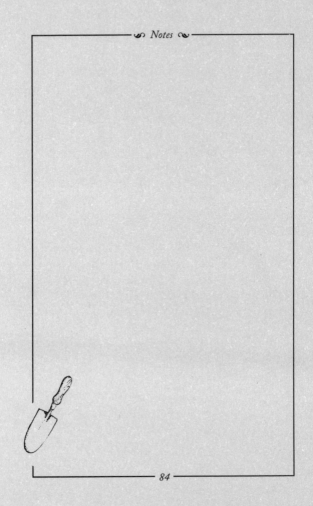

Winter Fragrance

*I*n the winter garden, scented plants are scarce, making the few that do exist particularly precious. The Ancient Greeks, the Assyrians, and the Romans knew this, and they grew violets, which, depending on the weather conditions, can be found in flower from late fall through late spring. In cottage gardens, violets were popular, not only for their pretty purple flowers and heart-shaped leaves, but also for their cooling, soothing, properties.

❧❧

Winter heliotrope *(Petasites fragrans)* and butterbur *(P. hybridus)* also have flowers that will perfume the winter garden. If you have a shaded, boggy area in the garden, where their rather invasive roots can be allowed to spread freely, both of these plants will reward you with clusters of sweetly scented flowers in late winter. The flowers appear before the foliage, which doesn't unfold until spring, when it covers the ground with large, round leaves. The Victorians grew these plants in pots indoors, where they would remain in bloom for many weeks.

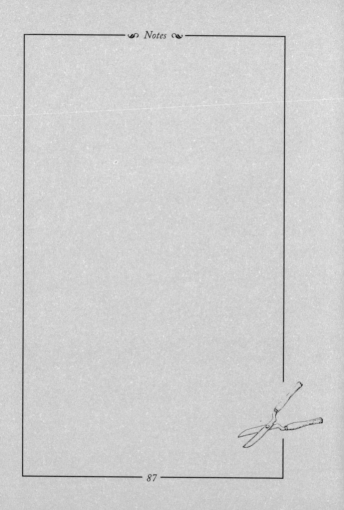

Sweet Peas

*F*or summer scent, few plants can beat climbing sweet peas *(Lathyrus odoratus)*, which can be trained to grow up a wigwam of canes or twiggy sticks in the vegetable or flower garden. Before you construct the wigwam, spade the ground well, and add plenty of well-rotted garden compost or manure. Set the sweet peas out in late spring, and tie in the young growth to the canes or sticks, until the plants are vigorous enough for their tendrils to support them. The best thing about sweet peas is, the more often you cut the flowers, the more the plants will produce.

❧❧

*D*on't confuse perennial, or everlasting, peas with sweet peas. Perennial peas come up every year, and are much stronger and more vigorous plants than annual sweet peas. They are very useful for covering unsightly boundaries or outhouses. They don't have the wide range of colors that sweet peas have, and, sadly, they have no fragrance, but they are attractive plants, and worth growing if you have space for them to scramble over a trellis, or a fence or wall.

*T*o have fragrance throughout the day and evening, mix the seeds of Virginian stock *(Matthiola maritima)* and night-scented stock *(Matthiola longipetala)*, and sow them in borders, around garden seats, and beneath windows. Sprinkle the seeds on well-prepared soil in mid-spring, and cover them lightly. Thin out the seedlings as they appear, to leave the plants about 9in (23cm) apart. Water them well in dry weather. Virginian stock is the more attractive of the two, but from mid- to late summer, night-scented stock is unbeatable for its fragrance.

&*&

Evening Fragrance

*A*s the daytime temperature begins to fall, there are some plants that open their blooms to attract night-flying moths and insects which pollinate by the light of the moon rather than the sun. These are among the most fragrant of all flowers, and their ghostly appearance in the half-light gives them an almost magical quality.

> *"Twas midnight—through the lattice wreath'd*
> *With Woodbine, many a perfume breath'd*
> *From plants that wake when others sleep,*
> *From timid jasmine buds, that keep*
> *Their odour to themselves all day,*
> *But, when the sunlight dies away,*
> *Let the delicious secret out*
> *To every breeze that roams about."*

Thomas Moore, 18th Century, Ireland.

*T*he evening primrose comes into its own at dusk, producing pale yellow, ethereal flowers with a rich scent.
Each flower opens only once, then withers and dies as
the sun rises, only to be replaced by another flower the
following evening. Evening primroses are self-seeding
biennials, and once established they will pop up all over
the garden.

꙰꙰

Some plants carry a clue to their perfume in their names. One such plant is sweet Cicely *(Myrrhis odorata)*, whose fragrance is reminiscent of myrrh. It is a handsome perennial, which can reach a height of 5ft (1.8m), and has deeply dissected leaves, rather like those of a fern. In some places, it is known as sweet fern. Old beekeepers would rub sweet Cicely leaves over the insides of the hives to entice the bees inside. The roots and leaves, and the seeds, which have a delicate, anise flavor, were used in the kitchen and as medicine. The seeds were also used to make a furniture polish that produced a deep, scented shine.

❧❧

Oswego Tea

$\mathcal{N}$o cottage garden should be without a clump of Oswego tea/bergamot *(Monarda didyma)*. It is an excellent plant for attracting bees and butterflies into the garden. The deep-crimson, thistle-like flowers appear in midsummer and last until early fall. The leaves, stems, and roots give off a wonderful aroma when they are crushed, and the plant is widely used in perfumery and for making potpourri. Oswego tea is also the name given to the aromatic infusion that is made from its leaves. The plant was named *Monarda*, after Dr. Nicholas Monardes of Seville, who included it in his Herbal of 1569, *Joyful Newes out of the Newe Founde Worlde*. It acquired the name bergamot, by which it is most commonly known in England, because its fragrance is similar to that of the bergamot orange, an Asian citrus fruit. Oswego tea is a native of North American woodlands, and needs a cool, moist soil, in partial shade. It will grow to a height of about 4ft (1.2m).

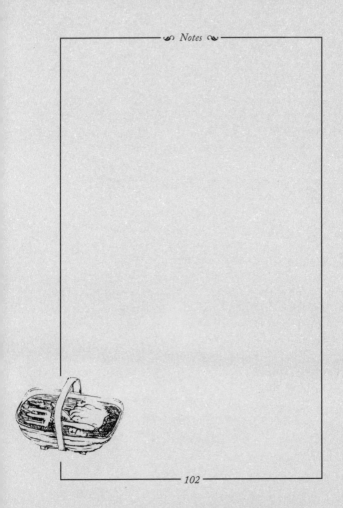

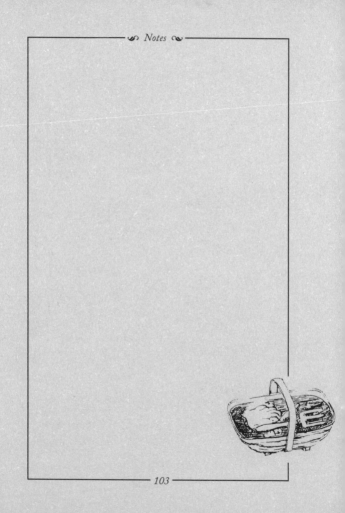

∾ *Notes* ∾

CHAPTER FOUR

Plants for Cooking and Eating

*I*n a small cottage garden where space is at a premium, everything must earn its keep, which is why cottage gardeners have always grown plants that not only look good, but are also good to eat.

Globe Artichokes

*O*ne plant that is as ornamental as it is edible is the tall and stately globe artichoke. The problem is that, when the heads begin to appear you have to decide whether to cut them off for the kitchen or leave them to develop into dramatic, thistlelike flowers. The answer, of course, is to grow some for cutting and some for the border too. Globe artichokes are easy to grow—in winter, dig in plenty of garden compost, set the plants out in midspring, 3ft (1m) apart, and keep them well watered. To encourage larger heads, take off the flower buds in the first year—in the second year, the heads will be ready for harvesting. The plants will produce flowers for up to six years, but the best heads for eating are those from two- or three-year-old plants.

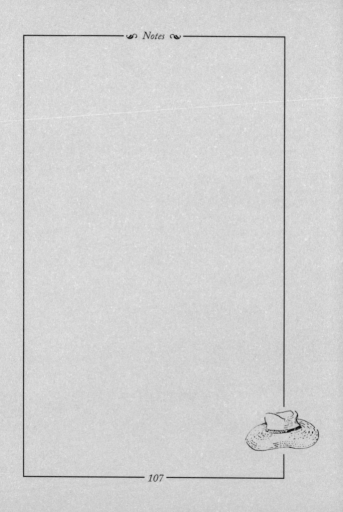

Rhubarb

Although it is a vegetable, most people consider rhubarb to be a fruit. It wasn't until around 1800 that cottagers discovered, possibly by accident, that rhubarb made a delicious filling for tarts and pies. Until then, they grew it for medicinal purposes only. It is a vigorous plant and looks very impressive in a larger cottage garden. It is best grown in a separate bed at least 3ft (1m) square, to prevent it from swamping other plants, but the colorful stems make it well worth the space it needs.

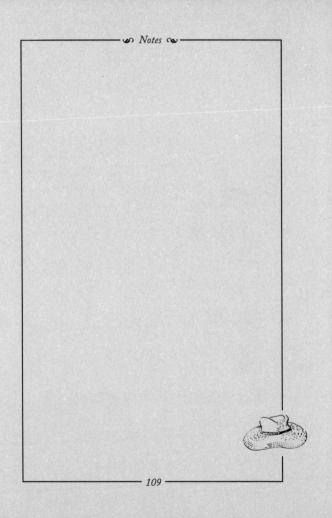

Fruit

Traditional cottage garden fruits included apples, pears, plums, and soft fruits, such as grapes, raspberries, and strawberries. Grapes were trained on south-facing walls or over pergolas, while berries were often grown as hedges to make the most of limited space. You can train fruit trees in a number of different ways; you can attach wires to walls to take fan-trained or espaliered trees, whose branches create attractive patterns. (These methods of growing are particularly suitable for apple, apricot, peach, and pear trees, and make the most of a sunny aspect.) If there are no substantial walls or fences in the garden, you can grow cordon trees supported on a sturdy post-and-wire fence. Cordons are single-stemmed plants, usually grown at a 45° angle to the ground to maximize the available space. French gardeners have a long tradition of training fruit trees, and grow them in many intricate patterns.

*T*he strawberries we know today were bred from two American species of Fragaria in the 18th century. Today's varieties either fruit once in summer or continuously from summer to fall. The latter are known as perpetual or ever-bearing strawberries. Cottage gardeners usually grow strawberries in rows, protecting the delicate fruit from the soil by covering the ground with straw or special strawberry mats. They like a fertile humus-rich soil and plenty of sun when the fruits are ripening. Strawberries are easy to grow in pots and barrels as well as in the open garden.

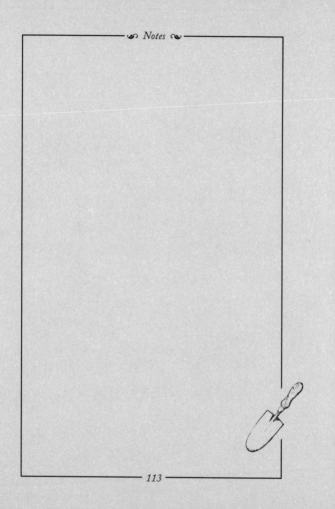

Salad Greens

Salad crops were probably grown in gardens long before flowers, fruits, or vegetables. In 1400, a short verse entitled *The Feate of Gardening* listed almost 100 commonly grown plants, including garlic, lettuces, onions, mustard, radishes, and salad burnet *(Sanguisorba minor)*, and by the 1500s, the list had expanded to include cress, chicory, cucumbers, purslane *(Portulaca oleracea)*, arugula / rocket *(Eruca vesicara)*, and sorrel. Many of these plants seem very sophisticated, even by today's standards, but it is likely that they were grown in the humblest of cottage gardens.

Sorrel is delicious, and very easy to grow. It was probably first discovered by field laborers who ate the leaves, which have a cooling, slightly acidic taste, to quench their thirsts. Sow the seeds in spring, then thin out the seedlings to 12in (30cm) apart. The young leaves are the tastiest, but use them sparingly, as a flavoring rather than as a substitute for lettuce. The larger leaves can be used to make sorrel soup. The plant is perennial, so you will not need to re-sow every year.

Radishes

*T*oday, we use radishes as a salad ingredient, but the Elizabethans ate them as an hor d'oeuvre, with salt and bread, because they were thought to stimulate the appetite. They are best eaten young and crisp—so sow little and often, and lift the roots before they become old and woody. Radishes make a good intercrop between rows of other vegetables, such as peas, which take longer to mature.

Beans

When choosing vegetables for the cottage garden, it is a good idea to go for those that not only taste good, but are ornamental too. Pole and bush beans are available in hundreds of different varieties, but for looks, choose those that have either pretty flowers or colorful pods, such as the purple-podded bush beans, which turn green when they are cooked. Grow pole beans up a teepee of hazel sticks or trellis in the flower border to create height and interest.

❧❧

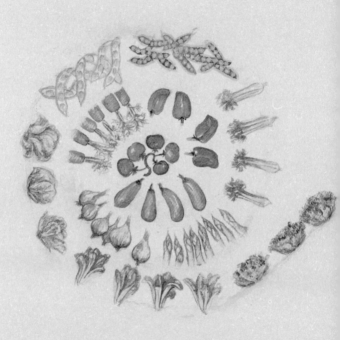

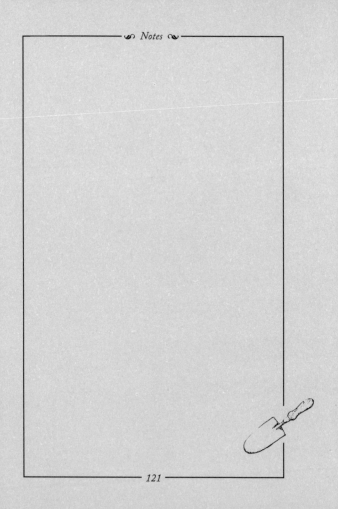

Herbs

*H*erbs never look out of place in the cottage garden, and although they don't need to be grown in a separate bed, for culinary herbs it is a good idea to use a small patch of ground that is within easy reach of the kitchen door, if you can. Prepare the ground by removing any weeds and dig in some horticultural grit to improve the drainage if the soil is heavy. Most culinary herbs, such as sage, sweet marjoram *(Origanum majorana)*, and thyme need warmth if they are to thrive, so choose a position where they will be in full sun for most of the day.

❦❧

*I*n most cottage gardens, herbs were grown among the flowers, and there are many that make good border subjects. Hyssop *(Hyssopus officinalis)* is a good choice, with its narrow, semievergreen leaves and blue flowers which bees love. Sage looks good in the flower border too, particularly the purple-leaved variety *S. o.* 'Purpurascens', and the variegated *S. o.* 'Tricolor'.

As a decorative, edible plant, fennel *(Foeniculum vulgare)* is hard to beat. It grows to a height of 6ft (2m), with a haze of feathery foliage and soft, yellow flowers in midsummer. There is also a bronze variety, *F. v.* 'Purpureum', with dark, burnished foliage which looks magnificent in a decorative border. Fennel has many uses in the kitchen—you can add the fresh leaves to sauces or cook them with fish, and you can cook the stems or grate them raw into salads. The seeds have a strong anise flavor, and are used to decorate bread and cakes. They will also allay hunger—Puritan churchgoers would carry handfuls of fennel seeds to eat during their long religious services, which gained them the nickname "meetin' seed."

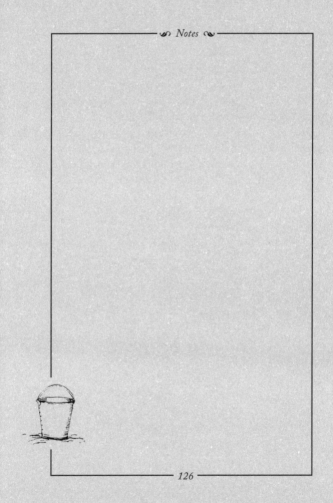

*B*orage is an annual herb that self-seeds freely. Some gardeners consider the plant, with its coarse, hairy leaves and stems, to be an intrusive weed, but its bright blue flowers are very pretty and have many uses to the cottage gardener. They are very attractive to bees in search of nectar, and both the flowers and leaves can be used to decorate cool drinks on hot summer days. The young leaves have a cooling, cucumberlike flavor, and can be added to salads.

If you want to grow mint in the garden, but worry that it may spread and overrun other plants, grow it in terra-cotta pots. Mint roots spread by underground runners, and keeping them confined in pots restricts their growth. Replace the plants each year by taking root cuttings, then discarding the old roots. Each pot should provide more than enough leaves for the average household. Although most people grow only peppermint, there are very many other species and varieties, and it is worth growing pots of some of the more usual ones, such as applemint *(M. suaveolens)*, eau-de-cologne mint (*M. piperita* 'Citrata'), or ginger mint (*M.* x *piperita*).

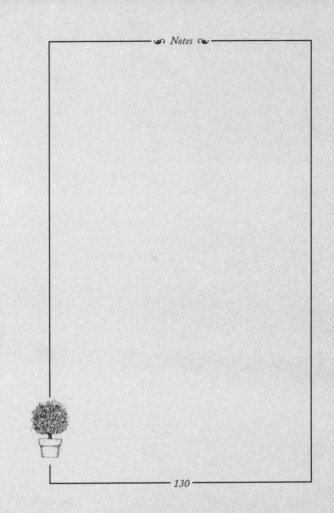

*C*oriander *(Coriandrum sativum)* has been grown in gardens for hundreds of years, and the whole plant is useful in the kitchen. The aromatic seeds have a sweet flavor, and are used in both sweet and savory dishes. The leaves are spicy and much used in Asian cookery. Coriander is easy to grow from seeds that you plant each year. Thin out the seedlings to about 10in (25cm) apart. The plants and seeds have a spicy aroma. Harvest the seed heads as soon as they begin to change color. A 16th century recipe suggests grinding together equal quantities of fennel and coriander seeds, and rubbing the mixture into pork before roasting.

❧

CHAPTER FIVE

Plants for Color

133

"One of the first things which all who care for gardens should learn, is the difference between true and delicate and ugly color..."
William Robinson, 1883

Color in the garden is a matter of personal preference. Some people feel more comfortable with soft, muted shades, while others set out to create a riot of color. Cottage gardeners of old didn't worry too much about color themes and combinations in their plantings–they planted the flowers that they liked and let them seed themselves around the garden, creating an impression of happy chaos. It was not until the late 19th and early 20th centuries, when William Robinson, Gertrude Jekyll, Vita Sackville-West, and others took up cottage gardening on a grand scale at their country homes, that color became recognized as an important feature of cottage garden design.

ও~

*I*n 1912, Gertrude Jekyll wrote: *"One can hardly go into the smallest cottage garden without learning or observing something new. It may be some two plants growing beautifully together by some happy chance, or a pretty tangle of mixed creepers...."* She took her ideas from small gardens and converted them to a country-garden scale–her house at Munstead Heath in Surrey, England had a flower border 200ft (60m) long and 14ft (4.5m) wide. Jekyll looked at gardens with the eye of an artist and planted borders with colors that flowed across the spectrum, starting with cool blues, mauves, and purples blending into pinks and whites, then exploding into reds and yellows. She used a huge range of plants–not only those that were thought of as country flowers, and her art was in blending humble soapwort *(Saponaria)*, lavender, and pinks with more exotic rhododendrons, cannas, and tender perennials.

*O*ne of Gertrude Jekyll's very subtle planting combinations, which you can copy in you own garden very easily, was to grow her own white columbine (then named *Aquilegia* 'Munstead White', but since renamed *Aquilegia* v. 'Nivea') with white foxgloves and peach-colored bellflowers *(Campanula persicifolia)*.

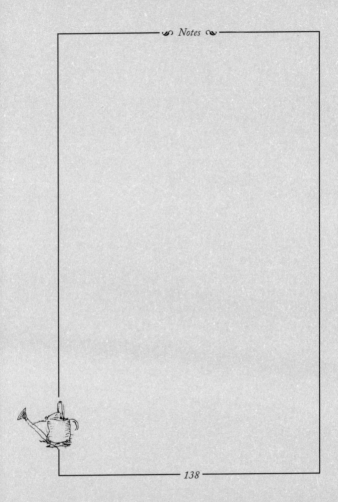

*W*illiam Robinson, in his classic book *The English Flower Garden*, expressed some strong ideas about color. *"Purple and lilac group well together,"* he wrote, *"but are best kept well away from red and pink; they do well with white and are at their best when surrounded with grey-white foliage."* He liked to use silver-leaved plants, such as senecio *(S. cineraria)* or snow-in-summer *(Cerastium tomentosum),* to edge clumps of purple flowers, but he warned that blue flowers required special treatment and strong blues should not be teamed with full yellows. We might agree with his first tip, but many gardeners today successfully team blue and yellow flowers. As always, it is a matter of personal preference for each gardener.

❧❧

*O*ne of William Robinson's particular dislikes was carpet bedding—the labor-intensive practice of growing tender plants from seeds and bedding them out in the garden in great swathes of color in spring and summer—only to take them all up again at the end of the season. Working cottage gardeners had neither the time nor the space for bedding, which was a style that originated in the gardens of the great stately homes of Victorian England, where armies of gardeners were employed to keep the borders constantly filled with colorful displays. *"A garish display of the greatest number of crudely contrasting colours,"* is how Robinson describes carpet bedding in his book, but in small areas, bedding plants can provide an instant, and inexpensive, effect. These days, you can buy young plants in "strips" or "plugs" from garden centers and use them to fill gaps in the beds, or in containers on the patio. For best effect, try to combine the colors tastefully—group together yellow marigolds, nasturtiums, and zinnias, for example, or cornflowers, heliotropes, and verbenas, with silver-leaved plants added for contrast.

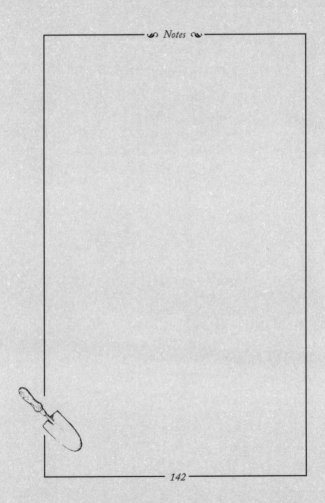

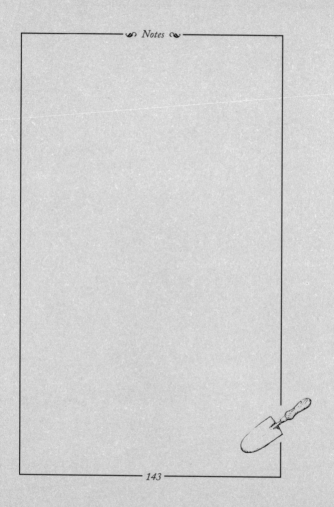

Notes

Summer Color

*F*or a short but colorful display in the borders, lupines are the choice of many cottage gardeners. The tall flower spikes in flaming red, pink, yellow, orange, blue, or white put on a grand show at the height of summer. Lupines are usually

grown as biennials sown from seeds in spring, and planted out in fall to flower the following year. Old-time cottagers grew them in rows for cutting, although the flowers don't last well indoors. They are better left in situ and staked to protect them from any unseasonal rain and wind.

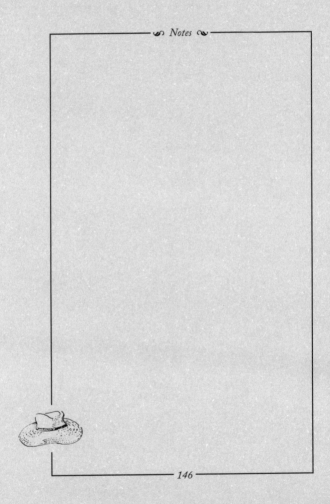

𝒱ictorian gardeners grew steeple bellflowers *(Campanula pyramidalis)* in pots on their windowsills, then stood the pots in the empty fireplaces to brighten them up in summer. These stately plants, which have 4ft (1.2m) tall spires of blue or white flowers were also known as chimney bellflowers.

❧☙

$\mathcal{P}$oppies *(Papaver)* are guaranteed to provide brilliant summer color. They vary widely, not just in color, but in habit and size too, ranging from the dainty, fleeting annual field poppy *(P. rhoeas)*, to the perennial oriental poppy *(P. orientale)*.

Oriental poppies make permanent features in the cottage garden with red, pink, or white flowers, all with the characteristic black blotching at the base. You can divide the clumps every few years to increase your stock of plants. Most other poppies are annuals, and once introduced into the garden, will seed themselves wherever they can. A particular favorite is the opium poppy *(P. somniferum)*, which is as old as civilization itself. It is well known for its narcotic properties, and according to classical mythology, was created by Somnus, the god of sleep. All parts of the plant are poisonous, except the seeds, which are widely used to decorate cakes and breads and pressed to produce a salad oil. Opium poppies are available in many shades of red, pink, and white, and can be grown in most garden soils. For a change of color plant Iceland poppies *(P. nudicaule)*, which come in shades of orange, yellow, and white. They make good cut flowers, with their papery, translucent flower heads held on slender stems.

Fall Color

*F*rom late summer onward, the cottage garden can be just as colorful as in the earlier part of the year. The late show starts with sunflowers *(Helianthus)*, with their huge, nodding heads on stems that can reach a height of 8 to 12ft (2.4-3.6m). Annual sunflowers *(H. annuus)* are the easiest to grow–simply sow clusters of two or three seeds in midspring, then, as the seedlings appear, take out the weakest to leave one strong plant from each group. If flowers 12ft (3.6m) high would be a problem in your garden, there are shorter cultivars that reach only 6ft (2m) or less, and dwarf varieties for pots and window boxes. Continue the sunshine theme with goldenrod *(Solidago)*, herbaceous perennials with arching plumes of soft, golden-yellow flowers that last until midfall. Goldenrod is attractive to bees and butterflies, and makes good cut flowers for window decorations. To take us into the latter part of fall, there are many species of coneflowers *(Rudbeckia)* which thrive in cottage gardens. One of the best known is Black-eyed Susan, with its golden ray-like petals and conspicuous dark cone in the center. The flowers of the variety 'Goldsturm' will bloom until the very last days of fall.

*O*ne of the oldest flowers of autumn is the saffron cro-cus *(C. sativus),* with its deep-purple, goblet-shaped flowers and narrow, gray-green leaves. Saffron, which is produced from the dried stigmas, is a precious com-modity–it takes more than 4,000 flowers to produce 1oz (25g) of saffron. Understandably, saffron produc-tion never became a cottage industry, but the flowers are welcome in midautumn and many gardeners grow them to provide a swathe of late color. Plant the corms in summer, in well-drained soil in a sunny position–they need plenty of warmth to ripen, and rarely do well in areas prone to cold, wet summers, but if you have the right conditions, you are in good com-pany–the clown in Shakespeare's *A Winter's Tale*, while mulling over his shopping list for the annual country fair, says: *"Let me see...what am I to buy for our sheep-shearing feast?... I must have saffron to colour the warden pies."* Warden pears, which originated in the little vil-lage of Warden in Bedfordshire in England, were great favorites for filling tarts at that time.

∾∾

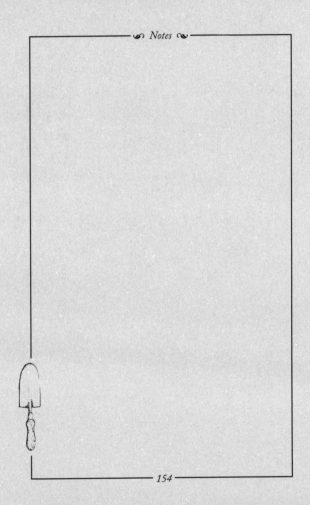

Winter Color

One of the secrets of a successful cottage garden is to plan your planting schemes so that you have something colorful in flower throughout the year. For winter color, plant early-flowering bulbs, such as irises *(I. reticulata)*, crocuses *(C tomassinianus)*, which are sometimes called old Tommies, and snowdrops under shrubs, such as daphne and wintersweet *(Chimonanthus praecox)*, that will flower throughout the winter. The bulbs can be supplemented with Christmas roses *(Helleborus niger)*, lungworts *(Pulmonaria)*, and violets, which will fill the gap before spring is really under way.

ᔥᔥ

Spring Color

A traditional cottage-garden planting for spring was a combination of powderblue forget-me-nots *(Myosotis)* and pink tulips. This is very effective in a narrow border at the foot of the house wall or as edging for a path. For best results, plant the tulips behind the forget-me-nots. As a variation on this theme, you could plant pink and white double daisies in place of the forget-me-nots.

*F*or a bold, bright, spring display, set out dwarf narcissus bulbs in a random pattern among miniature wallflowers in fall. The resulting show will be a rich tapestry of velvety reds, burnt oranges, and brilliant yellows. To achieve the same effect on a larger scale, plant full-sized daffodils and wallflowers. For a more sophisticated look in early summer, plant ornamental onions *(Allium sphaerocephalon),* which have wine-colored flowers, among creamy white perennial masterwort *(Astrantia major)* in fall.

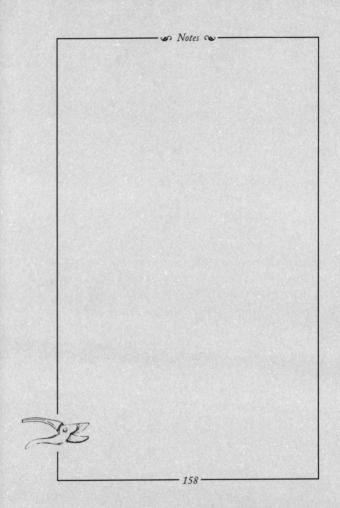

Like many gardeners of her day, Vita Sackville-West, who created a cottage garden on a grand scale at Sissinghurst Castle in Kent, England, was trying to incorporate cottage garden principles into a large plot. She did this by splitting the garden into a series of outdoor "rooms," each of which captured something of the romance of the cottage garden. The secret of her success was in lavish planting, which filled every available inch (centimeter) of soil with a profusion of plants, and every wall space with lush climbers. She favored all the traditional cottage plants—herbs, lilies, pinks, primroses, and old-fashioned shrub roses, but she supplemented these with any exotic plants that fitted her idea of a romantic, cottagey look.

$\mathscr{W}$riting from Sissinghurst Castle in the winter of 1949, Sackville told her readers that she was endeavoring to make a gray-and-white garden. The rectangular bed she had earmarked for the purpose was surrounded by a high yew hedge, a wall, and a strip of boxwood hedging, and was divided in half by a path of flagstones. Here she visualized a sea of silvery foliage–lavender cotton, southernwood, *(Artemisia abrotanum)*, and lamb's ear *(Stachys byzantina)*, punctuated by tall, white, regal lilies, irises, and white peonies. *"This is an experiment which I ardently hope may be successful ... I cannot help hoping that the great ghostly barn-owl will sweep silently across a pale garden next summer–the pale garden that I am now planting..."* Almost fifty years later, the White Garden at Sissinghurst is famous the world over.

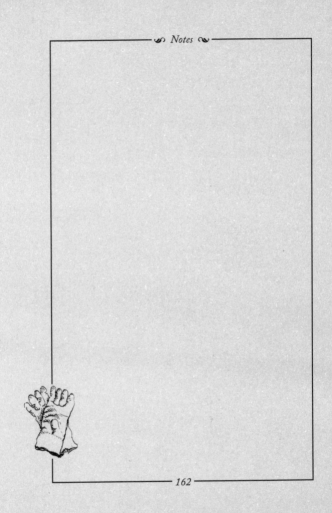

CHAPTER SIX

Facts and Folklore

Please note that although many people swear by herbal remedies today, those mentioned here are for interest only, and it is not recommended that you should experiment with them. Herbal medicines can be very strong, and should be taken only under the guidance of a qualified practitioner.

∽∾

The primary purpose of the cottage garden was to provide the cottager with food for his table and items for household use. The first gardens were full of plants that had many uses within the household. In the days before people could pop down to the local store for soaps, polishes, and detergents, the garden was the main source of household supplies. Similarly, medicine from a qualified doctor was an expensive commodity that many families could not afford, and the herbs and plants in the garden provided a host of remedies for everything from the common cold to corns on the feet. Some of the household uses for plants have stood the test of time, while others have been relegated to the realms of folklore, but all are of historical interest to today's cottage gardener.

Companion Planting

The old cottage gardeners did not have access to garden chemicals and pesticides, and had to develop their own methods of dealing with garden problems. Companion planting as a method of controlling pests and diseases is as old as gardening itself, and has as much relevance today as it did hundreds of years ago. The idea that certain plants can help one another when they are planted together has many adherents, and even if, in many cases, the theories can't be scientifically proven, companion planting is a tradition that has been handed down through generations of gardeners.

~~~

If you don't like the idea of using chemicals in the garden, why not try your hand at companion planting? Organic gardeners know that the best pest-beaters are the natural ones—hoverflies, lacewings, and ladybugs (ladybirds). To attract these useful insects, edge the vegetable patch with clumps of marigolds. The beneficials will fly into this colorful border and find plenty of aphids and other pests on the neighboring vegetables.

*A*ll members of the Allium family, including chives *(A. schoenoprasum)* and garlic *(A. sativum)*, make good companions for roses. The aroma of the onion-flavored leaves is believed to deter aphids, and the flowers of chives or Welsh onions *(A. fistulosum)* make a very pleasing display beneath the bushes.

❧❧

*W*allflowers planted at the base of an apple tree not only look good, but will attract pollinating insects to work on the blossom, ensuring a good crop of fruit.

❧❧

*O*ne of the best plants for attracting beneficial insects is meadow foam (*Limnanthes douglasii*), with its open-faced cream and yellow flowers. Planted along the edge of a vegetable garden or beneath fruit bushes, rows of meadow foam plants look very attractive.

Research has shown that if you alternate rows of brassicas with rows of legumes, pests—such as the cabbage root fly—find it difficult to target the plants because they become confused by the smell of the surrounding vegetables. Another piece of old cottage garden advice is to work in the vegetable plot after sunset, when there is less chance of attracting carrot fly.

To deter cabbage white butterflies from laying their eggs on brassica plants, surround the bed with peppermint *(M. piperita)*—the aroma will disguise the smell of the cabbages. Hyssop is said to have the same effect.

Cottage gardeners used a range of plants, such as wormwood *(Artemesia absinthium)*, tansy *(Tanacetum vulgare)*, and catnip *(Nepeta cataria)*, all of which have strong aromas, to deter aphids and other pests. Some of these plants were used to deal with indoor pests too. Wormwood was known to repel fleas, as this 16th-century verse states quite graphically:

"Where chamber is sweeped, and wormwood is strowne,
    No flea for his life dare abide to be knowne."

Southernwood is a close relative of wormwood, but it has an even more powerful aroma, and was used in nosegays and for strewing on the cottage floor to combat household smells. Even today, southernwood is dried and included in insect-repellent sachets. It is particularly effective against moths.

Growing plants to attract bees was second nature to early cottagers. Any plant that was useful to bees found a place in the garden. The first bee plants, such as wild thyme, scabious, knapweeds, and deadnettles, were wild plants introduced from the countryside, but they were soon followed by borage, lavender, red valerian, and a host of others. To be productive, bees must have access to a succession of nectar and pollen plants from early spring to late fall. For spring pollen, grow early crocuses, bluebells *(Hyacinthoides)*, forget-me-nots, and lungworts. For summer, the choice is vast, but bell-flowers, globe thistles *(Echinops)*, honeysuckle, and thrift are excellent. Later in the year, bees like to work the fall-flowering colchicum *(C. autumnale)*, golden-rod, stonecrop *(Sedum)*, and teasels.

∽∾

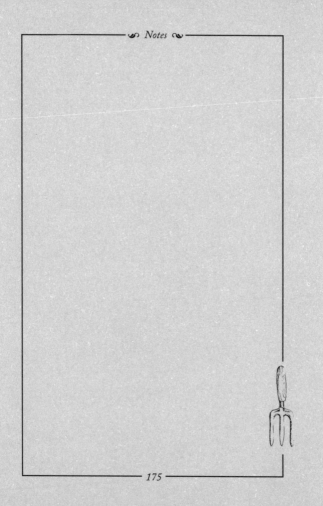

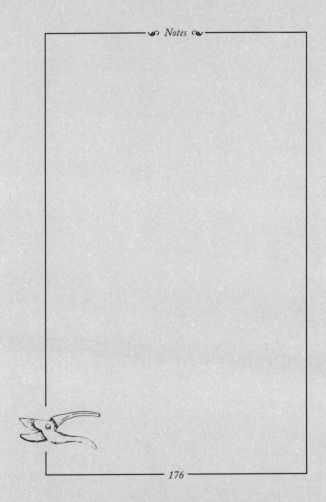

Before the advent of soap, travelers and settlers carried the seeds and roots of soapwort wherever they roamed. They would plant this easily grown perennial where they settled, which is why it has naturalized so freely in country areas. The leaves had to be crushed, boiled in water, and then strained to produce a liquid that made just about enough lather for bathing and for washing clothes. When the travelers moved on, soapwort—or bouncing Bet, as it is known in many parts of North America—was left to grow wild. It has a lovely, unkempt, blowsy appearance that suits the cottage garden style perfectly and fragrant, pink flowers that last from midsummer through fall.

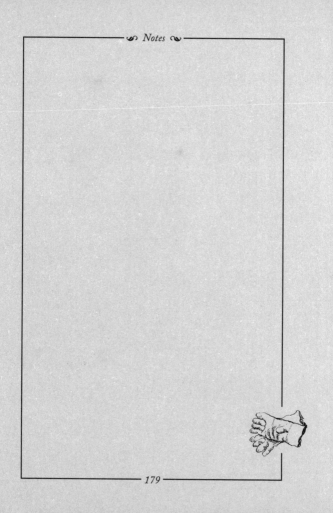

*F*or medicinal purposes, no cottage garden was without a clump of heliotrope *(Valeriana officinalis)*. With its pale pink flower clusters above a mass of fresh green foliage, it is still widely grown as an ornamental plant, but its medicinal properties have all but been forgotten. One of the plant's common names was all-heal, and the roots were collected to make strong tinctures for all maladies of the head, from the mildest headache to hysteria. It should not be confused with red valerian, another very common cottage-garden plant that cheerfully seeds itself around the garden, particularly on and around old stone walls, but has no medicinal value.

ॐॐ

Notes

*T*he larkspur *(Consolida)*, or lark's heel, as country people call it, was once thought to possess properties for strengthening eyesight. *C. ambigua* was used to make an eyewash, but like its close relatives, the delphiniums, most parts of the plant are poisonous. You can grow larkspur from seeds in spring, and it makes a good cut flower with its tall, stately spires of pink, white, or lavender-blue flowers.

∽∾

*O*ne plant that found a place in every garden, because of its medicinal properties, was betony *(Stachys officinalis)*. The Romans used the leaves to purify the blood, and in medieval times it was used to alleviate no less than forty-seven different ailments. Betony sometimes goes by the name of bishopswort, probably because it was widely grown in monastery gardens. There are white- and pink-flowered forms, and they both make compact, late-flowering plants for the front of the border or as a path edging.

∽∾

The old cottagers were always on the lookout for drinks and potions that could be made from plants. One old recipe is for gale beer, made from sweet gale, or bog myrtle *(Myrica gale)*, a shrub that grows in damp areas and has a sweet, resinous aroma. Before hops were widely used to make beer, boiling water was poured on the leaves of sweet gale, then honey was added, and the mixture was left to ferment naturally in wooden casks. Sprigs of the shrub were also laid among bed linen to drive away moths and fleas.

❧❧

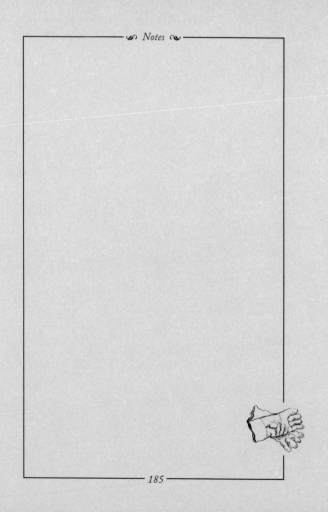

*I*n shady gardens, it is often possible to find a patch of wood sorrel *(Oxalis acetosel-la)*, a tiny, white-flowered plant with shamrock-shaped leaves. We think of it now as a decorative plant for woodland gardens, but its leaves were eaten as a salad vegetable as early as the 15th century, although it has a rather sharp taste and is not good for the body in large quantities. Native Americans fed it to their horses, because they believed it increased their speed. It has also been associated with the Druids, who adopted it as their emblem. Despite this mixed heritage, it makes a pretty little spreading plant for a damp, shady part of the garden.

*T*here are many conflicting tales in cottage garden folklore about how sweet William got its name, and many nationalities claim the plant as their own. Some say it was named after William the Conqueror, who invaded England in 1066, while others say it comes from St. William of Rochester, who lived in the 12th century. Still others say it was discovered by Carthusian monks traveling in eastern Europe. It had certainly reached England by 1553, when Henry VIII ordered bushels of the plants for his new Hampton Court Palace garden. Some claim it

was named after William, Duke of Cumberland, "The Butcher of Culloden," who defeated the Scots in 1746, and in some parts of Scotland the plant is called stinking Willie. In Ulster, sweet Williams are associated with King William III. Whatever the origins of its common name, the plant is a member of the Dianthus family, and an easily grown cottage-garden biennial with a bold, bouncy appearance. Once established, it will seed itself freely around the garden. The distinctive red and white markings on the densely packed, flattened flower heads do not always find favor with those who like their flowers in discrete pastel shades, but it has always been popular with cottager gardeners.

*M*uch of the cottage gardeners' folklore revolves around the winter plants, holly, ivy, and mistletoe. Winter is filled with festivities that demand a good supply of evergreen foliage and berries, and of these, mistletoe is the most precious. Cottage gardeners should be delighted to find it growing on the boughs of old apple or pear trees, and, contrary to popular belief, it does no damage to the trees. Bringing a piece of mistletoe indoors is supposed to bring luck and encourage fertility–thus the tradition of kissing beneath the mistletoe.

The holly tree is so entwined in folklore, standing for protection against evil, and acting as a sentinel to ward off demons and witches, that no cottage garden should be without it. The branches, with their dark leaves and contrasting bright berries, were brought indoors during winter festivals to deal with those troublesome goblins that rushed around the house unseen, turning milk sour, and spreading infections. Where holly goes then ivy must go too–the two plants are inextricably bound together as illustrated in the old Christmas carol *The Holly and the Ivy*.

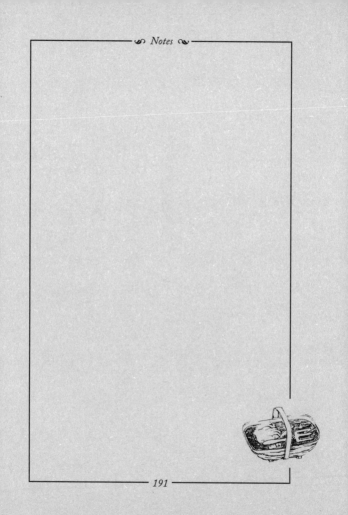

*F*oxgloves have made an almost seamless transition from natural woodland clearings into cultivated gardens. The deep purple spikes of the wild species have given way to garden hybrids in shades of pink, apricot, cream, or white, but all have the characteristic spotting inside the tubular flowers. In folklore, the foxglove has all sorts of supernatural connotations, probably because the plant is poisonous and is used in the pharmaceutical industry to produce the drug digitalis. The tubular flowers acquired the name foxgloves from the belief that foxes donned them to enable them to creep up silently on unsuspecting cottagers and steal their chickens. The juice of the plant was believed to keep away bad spirits, and to bring back children who had been snatched by the fairies. Foxgloves are very easy to grow if you give them a partly shaded position in a fairly moist soil. They are very popular with bees, who disappear inside the flowers to extract nectar and pollen.

One of the most aptly named plants must surely be travelers joy *(Clematis vitalba)*, a common cottage-garden climber. It was discovered by 16th-century herbalist and botanist John Gerard, who saw it growing in every hedgerow. He marveled at the shade it offered to weary travelers, and wrote, *"thereupon, I have named it Traveller's Joy."* The plant has an even older name—old man's beard—which refers to the shaggy seedheads that appear in fall. Long ago, poor people would cut the woody stems and smoke them like tobacco, and the plant soon acquired the nickname boy's bacca, or poor man's bacca.

ↄↄ

Rosemary *(Rosemarinus officinalis)* has a long tradition as a useful cottage garden plant, dating back to long before sprigs were thrown on the barbecue to flavor roasting meat. An herbal of 1525 said that leaves spread under the pillow would *"deliver one from evil dreams,"* and a book entitled *The Garden of Health,* written in 1579, recommended that carrying the flower would *"make thee merry, glad, gracious and well-beloved of all men."* In one recipe book, rosemary was recommended as a mouthwash for bad breath.

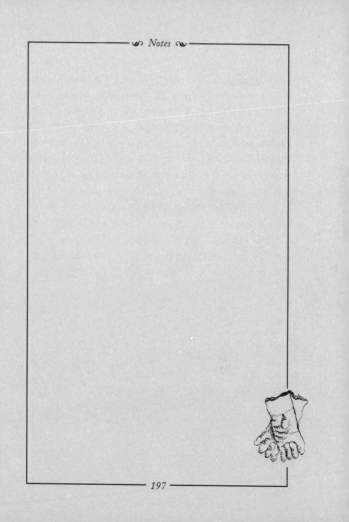

*I*n contrast to rosemary, rue *(Ruta graveolens)* is the herb of sadness, pity and repentance. Shakespeare called it the *"sour herb of grace,"* and in his play *Richard II*, the gardener plants a bank of rue in the grounds of Pontefract Castle, in the place were the Queen had shed tears. Rue has aromatic leaves, but the fragrance cannot really be described as pleasant, and the foliage may cause allergic skin reactions in some people. It was, nevertheless, dried and strewn on floors to combat household smells, and, being bitter and strong, was believed to guard against witches. Inn-keepers would give sprigs of rue to travelers to keep them safe on their onward journeys.

ꔫꔫ

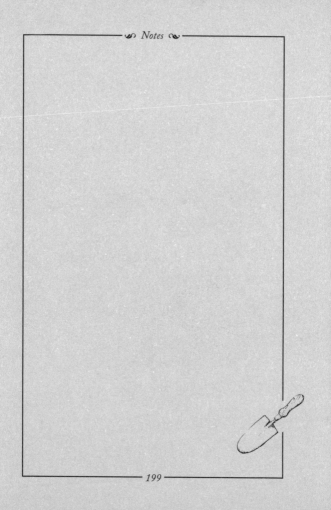

CHAPTER SEVEN

Plants for Pleasure

*T*hese days, many of us use our gardens primarily for relaxation and pleasure, and prefer to fill our borders with all our favorite flowers, rather than strive to be self-sufficient in fruit and vegetables. The plants in this chapter are those that are grown mainly because they look good. Some of them need a little more care than others, but they are all worth growing for the extra pleasure they give.

*C*ottage gardeners of old, who had the space and time, grew flowers for their looks, as well as plants for the kitchen and the medicine cabinet. In the 18th century, gardeners who bred and developed flowers for show became known as "florists". The list of approved florist's flowers included auricula primulas, pinks, polyantha primulas, ranunculus, and tulips. Ordinary country men and women developed plant breeding to a very high level, and the challenge of producing flowers that were ever brighter, bolder, and more perfect took hold in the public imagination.

Tulips

Tulips reached Europe from Turkey in the 16th century and sparked a love affair that lasted centuries. The heyday of the tulip was the late 18th century, when one catalog listed seven hundred different varieties. Particularly prized were the "Bizarre" tulips–those affected by a virus disease that caused the color to break and form streaks, feathering, and stripes. These tulips could be propagated only by offsets from each bulb, and as a result, the price of bulbs soared. Sometimes they changed hands for hundreds of pounds and, as "Tulipmania" gripped Europe, buying tulips became as risky as dealing in the art world. Most cottage gardeners could not afford to cash in on this craze, and they continued to cultivate "cottage" tulips–less-showy, single-colored blooms that have stood the test of time. However, you shouldn't rule out some of the new tulip varieties, which are perfectly suited to the cottage garden, particularly the peony-flowered types, which have a soft, relaxed appearance, and the many dwarf varieties that are ideal for growing in window boxes.

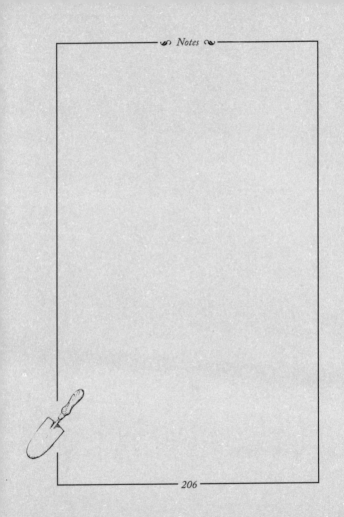

∽ *Notes* ∾

Primroses

Primroses are some of the best-loved cottage-garden plants, and they owe much of their success to a penniless pianist from Gresham, Oregon. In the early 1930s, Florence Bellis moved to a leaky timber barn on Johnson's Creek, and with just a few packets of seeds from Sutton's in England, began developing a strain of polyanthus-type primroses. Her plants, which she pollinated by the light of an oil lamp with only a woodburning stove for warmth, became highly sought after for their jewellike colors, sweet scent, and hardy nature. The name of Barnhaven, her cabin home, is still recognized the world over as the standard-bearer for cottage-garden primroses.

Cottage primroses need to be grown in rich, moist soil, and do best in a position that is shaded from the full heat of the sun. Buy young plants in fall, and set them out immediately. Primroses will last for many years, and older plants can be divided and replanted in late spring, after they have flowered.

Dahlias

*F*or a late-summer show of flowers, many cottage gardeners chose dahlias, which were hugely popular in the 19th century, and are enjoying something of a revival today. The old favorites–doubles and show dahlias–have given way to a range of decorative and cactus-flowered forms, ranging in size from the smallest dwarfs, to giants growing to over 6ft (2m). If you want to grow dahlias, visit garden centers and flower shows toward the end of summer, and make a list of the varieties you like best. They grow from tubers that must be lifted and stored in a frost-free place in winter. Plant out the tubers in late spring, when all danger of frost has passed. Dahlias are relatively trouble free, and apart from watering, and staking the taller varieties, are easy to grow. When they come into flower you can enjoy them in the garden, or cut them for indoor arrangements. Remove the faded blooms to prolong flowering.

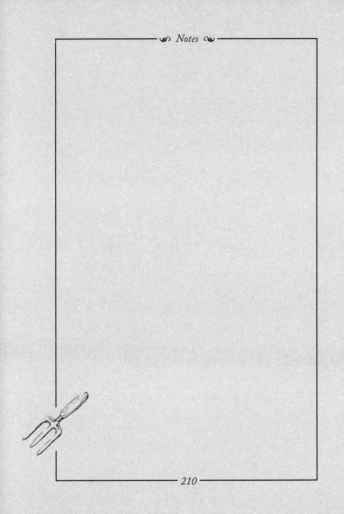

Pansies

The pansy is another old cottage-garden favorite. The one first grown in cottage gardens was the heartsease pansy *(Viola tricolor)*, forever associated with love and affairs of the heart. This is the plant whose juice was squeezed into Titania's eyes in Shakespeare's *A Midsummer Night's Dream,* to make her fall in love with the ass-headed Bottom. The name pansy comes from the French *pensee*, and, as Shakespeare put it, *"that's for thoughts."* It was this little three-colored flower that inspired generations of breeders to produce the bigger, bolder, faced pansies.

The most significant introduction to modern gardens must be the winter-flowering pansy *(V.* x *wittrockiana)*, which flowers almost constantly throughout the year, and is particularly attractive in hanging baskets and containers. The old violas, however, have not been forgotten, and many of the original, daintier types are still available including *Viola.* 'Jackanapes', a bicolored variety said to be named after Jekyll's donkey, Jack—a member of the menagerie she kept at her Surrey home.

Roses

*F*or sheer, unadulterated pleasure, there is little to beat the cottage-garden rose. The first roses in cottage gardens were probably grown from cuttings or hips taken from the wild hedgerow rose, eglanteria (also called sweet briar or eglantine) which has been grown in gardens since the 16th century, and is still widely grown today for its fresh fragrance and clear, pink flowers in early summer. Most of its fragrance comes not from the flowers but from the young leaves, which give off a wonderful scent after a shower of rain. Eglanteria has arching stems that lend themselves to being trained over a porch or arbor. It can also be grown as an informal hedge, where its thorny stems make an effective barrier, and its bright red hips make a good show in fall. It will tolerate a fairly poor soil and does not need the care and pruning that many modern roses require. All it needs is a light pruning at the beginning of spring to remove any weak stems or straggly growth.

*I*f you want a climber for growing against the house wall, look no further than the old glory rose, *Rosa* 'Gloire de Dijon'. Bred in France in the mid 19th century, it has become one of the best-loved cottage-garden roses, with its large, apricot-pink flowers that change color according to the weather—the warmer it is, the pinker they become. This rose will cover a bare wall, and has heavily scented blooms that appear very early in the summer, and sometimes reappear later in the year. It is fairly hardy, and can cope with even a shady wall. To keep it at its best, mulch the soil around the base with well-rotted manure in spring.

*T*here are no rules about which roses should be grown in a cottage garden, but the old-fashioned varieties and those with a softer, less-formal appearance look best. For the widest choice of species and cultivars, buy from a specialist nursery. In the cottage garden, roses are best grown in mixed borders with other flowering shrubs or trained to scramble over buildings and fences, rather than as isolated specimens in a rose bed. Good border companions for roses include purple-leaved sage, lavender cotton, and nepeta (*Nepeta* 'Six Hills Giant').

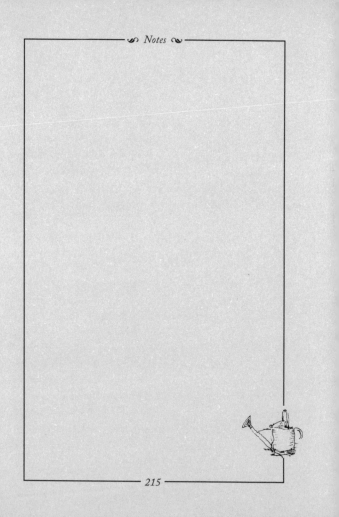

Lilies of the Valley

The fact that we grow plants for our personal enjoyment, and not simply to conform to someone else's idea of what should be grown, is illustrated by the melancholy poet, Samuel Coleridge. While other poets were enthusing over the cheerful colors of spring, he wrote: *"some flowers rush upon the eye with garish bloom...Not such art though, sweet Lily of the Vale!"* His passion was for the purity of the sweetly scented, nodding heads of lily of the valley *(Convallaria majalis)*. Gardeners either love or hate this flower, and in some gardens it can give a disappointing show, usually because it is grown on a sun-baked rockery where it does very badly indeed. Lilies of the valley are happiest in a woodland environment, in moist, humus-rich soil and dappled shade. The ideal place for them is next to a mossy wall, which will keep their roots cool, or beneath a small tree, which will shade them from the summer sun. Cover the ground around the plants with a mulch of leaf mold or garden compost in spring each year, and they will spread naturally to form a fresh, green carpet of foliage topped by fragrant white flowers.

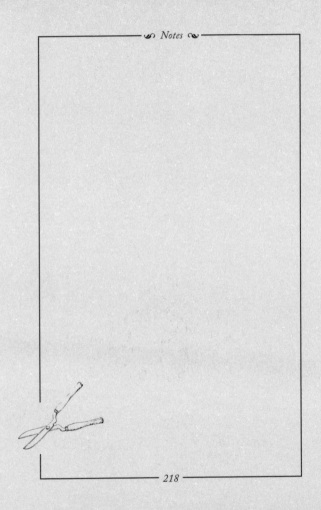

Hollyhocks

No flowers give a garden such an air of maturity as hollyhocks. They have been a feature of cottage gardens for hundreds of years, towering against white-washed walls or standing sentinel in open borders. Sown from seeds in late spring or early summer, they can be planted out in fall, and will produce stems up to 10ft (3m) tall during the following summer. The flowers come in red, yellow, and shades of pink, ranging from the palest apricot through lavender to deep maroon, and are very attractive to bees. Hollyhocks like a sunny position, and do best in soil that has been amended with well-rotted compost or manure. Water them regularly in hot weather. They are perennials, but they grow taller and produce fewer flowers each year, and they are also prone to a rust disease, so it is usually best to treat them as biennials. If you want to retain them, cut the stems down to 6in (15cm) above the ground after they have flowered.

Snowdrops

Snowdrops are the winter favorites of many gardeners, but they rarely make good cut flowers, because they flop and wilt very quickly. To help them last longer, plunge them up to their necks in cold water as soon as you cut them, and stand them in a cool place for 24 hours before you bring them indoors. That way, they will stand better when you arrange them, and you will be able to enjoy their scent for longer. Alternatively, lift a clump while the snowdrops are in flower, and place it in a terra-cotta or china bowl. Cover the soil with florist's moss, and keep it moist and cool. The snowdrops should bloom for almost as long as they would out-doors, and when they have finished flowering you can divide the clump and replant the pieces in the garden.

Flowers for Cutting

There should be no shortage of cutting material in a well-stocked cottage garden, particularly throughout spring and summer, when the borders are overflowing with flowers. The art of cottage-garden floristry is to cut the flowers when they are at their best and place them in plain pottery jugs, clear glass vases, or china bowls. There should be no need for florist's wire or foam—the more natural the look, the better. For spring, combine bluebells with sprigs of lilac *(Syringa)*, or the pink flowering currant *(Ribes sanguineum)*. Alternatively, pick sweet rocket *(Hesperis matronalis)* or primroses for their delicate scent. In summer, sweet peas always look fresh, and need no extra foliage in the vase. Sprigs of mock orange blossom look and smell wonderful when combined with old-fashioned pink roses such as *Rosa* 'Louise Odier' or 'Constance Spry'. White sprigs of gypsophila *(Gypsophila paniculata)* provide a classic country-style background to dainty, mauve scabious and blue love-in-a-mist.